EZRA POUND Po

EZRA POUND

Poems selected by THOM GUNN

faber and faber

First published in 2000
by Faber and Faber Limited
3 Queen Square London WC1N 3AU

Photoset by Parker Typesetting Service, Leicester
Printed in Italy

Thom Gunn is hereby identified as editor
of this work in accordance with Section 77
of the Copyright, Designs and Patents Act 1988

A CIP record for this book
is available from the British Library

ISBN 0–571–20430–9

10 9 8 7 6 5 4 3 2 1

Contents

2

3

4

Introduction

At the end of the twentieth century's first decade, Ezra Pound moved to London, a young American in his mid-twenties. He did so, he said, because he hoped to meet there the greatest living poet, W. B. Yeats. He succeeded in this fairly soon, and became a friend. He met, too, Thomas Hardy and Henry James, two living classics. England would also have been a source of poetic energy because of Robert Browning, twenty years dead but an influence deeper and more lasting on Pound than any of the others. Pound's was seldom a poetry of personal utterance until the Pisan Cantos of the 1940s, when the crisis of the prison-cage forced him into a new kind of writing. Meanwhile, Browning's dramatic poetry had taught Pound how to speak through the mouths of others: a troubadour-warrior, a Chinese river-merchant's wife, Sextus Propertius, or an Italian Renaissance prince. His first commercially published book was called *Personae* – persona being the name of the mask a Roman actor wore, thence coming to refer to the part played. It has since become a fashionable critical term – too fashionable, as if a poem is necessarily spoken through another voice than that of the author, but in Pound's case it usually was. He was willing to try any kind of voice, and at the same time he conducted an extensive apprenticeship translating, imitating, adapting, and inventing new kinds of versification. Even more than most young poets, he sought out what was available, and extended it in testing it.

In the course of his search, he almost inadvertently founded Imagism, a school consisting of his friend H.D., her husband, and himself, of which the most famous exemplary poem is his own 'In a Station of the Metro' (1913), consisting of two images that through juxtaposition constitute a visual comparison. The idea behind Imagism, at its simplest, and it always remained pretty simple, was this: the poet sees an image and has a reaction to it; the poet presents the image as vividly as possible on paper; then, without being told how to react, the reader reacts to the image in the same way as the poet. It was a tiny movement with a tiny life-span which produced tiny poems; but it was to be the most influential poetic movement of the century, in subject matter confining itself to the sensory at the expense of the conceptual, in style emphasizing clarity and compression, and in form carrying with it the implicit necessity of free verse, which was still young and experimental at that time, and by no means the drab norm it is nowadays.

The influence of Imagism was discernible on Pound's translations from the ancient Chinese, a group of poems published in 1915 as *Cathay*. At the time of writing, Pound knew no Chinese, but he had been entrusted with the notebooks of Ernest Fenollosa by his widow, who – clearly a woman of discrimination – could see a resemblance between their contents and the kind of thing that Pound was doing. Fenollosa had been an honoured American scholar of Japanese antiquities who had eventually decided to study ancient Chinese poetry (then little known in the West) and had taken tutorials from Japanese professors of Chinese, being conducted word by word through the originals to produce his own literal translation into English which Pound now proceeded to versify with sensitivity and intelligence. He reproduced in his versions a characteristic note of restrained wistfulness which echoes through the work of subsequent Western poets, from William Carlos Williams to Gary Snyder. Selected physical details did the job of emotion or thought. In 'Taking Leave of a Friend', the feeling is sufficiently implied by the imagery, so that overt expression of regret would be superfluous. This project produced its own kind of free verse, each line being heavily end-stopped and tending to consist of a distinct item parallel to those of other lines, as Donald Davie has pointed out. Other kinds of free verse were to be invented for other kinds of poem, improvised but definably different forms.

In *Homage to Sextus Propertius* (1917), the line is more garrulous, as is suitable to a poetry of wit, gossip, and opinion. The book is an arrangement of poems spliced together from the Latin of Propertius, translation as interpretation. In them Propertius becomes a dramatic character, as scornful of the Emperor Augustus' imperialism as Pound is of the British imperialism of his own time. It is a far from literal translation (the reader will readily notice the anachronistic frigidaires and Roman policemen in Tibet); and the voice of Propertius is at times lively, pompous, eloquent, pedantic, subtle, and broadly comic. The shifts in tone are occasionally puzzling. We may contrast the compressed power of poem VI with the opening lines of IX and wonder about the relationship, or lack of it: if the second of these is a parody, is it Propertius himself parodying somebody, or is it Pound's parody of Latin translation in English?

Toward the end of that marvellous first decade of publication, Pound started his most ambitious work, the *Cantos*, which was to occupy his poetic energies for the rest of his life. He called it an epic, but defined epic only as 'a poem containing history'. You might retort that a bag of groceries *contains*, but that the only relationship between its contents is in the needs of the person who purchased them. The *Cantos* contains – besides history – myth, anecdote, excerpts from many kinds of document, and even poems of various sorts that can stand on their own (for example 'Tudor indeed is gone'), a long-meditated translation from Cavalcanti, versions of Chinese landscape poems, and so on. What to make of all this assortment? The commentators who have found most continuity in the work as a whole have identified the poet with the Odysseus of the first Canto, adventuring and (in Pound's words) sailing after knowledge. Odysseus goes down to the underworld to give speech to the dead: the first line of the first Canto is 'And then went down to the ship', and the Canto itself is a translation of the eleventh book of the *Odyssey* – though from the Renaissance Latin of Andreas Divus, rather than from the original of Homer. How does a poet perceive what he explores while he explores it? Pound would answer 'not as land looks on a map/but as sea bord seen by men sailing' (Canto LIX). So here we are with Pound, translating the archaic into an archaic measure (that of 'The Seafarer'), and suddenly flipping through the pages in his volume, published in 1538, to a translation of a Homeric Hymn to Aphrodite – something as unexpected as the discovery round some unmapped point of a sheltered bay or a dangerous shoal on the coast. Unexpected but appropriate, in that he is sailing not only after knowledge but after beauty also, for Aphrodite is the goddess of beauty.

The Old English line becomes rhythmically looser, in the second Canto developing step by step into a new and flexible free verse line. The arrangement of subject matter was experimental, too: as in the early poem about the Paris Metro, the procedure is often to place one detail by another apparently unrelated, and expect the reader to make the connection. The connection is always easier to make on a rereading, in that we have meanwhile been able to work out a thematic core to each Canto, sometimes obvious and sometimes not. The second Canto centres on a metamorphosis out of Ovid – the boy-god hitching his way across the seas is Dionysus, requiring our worship, might we say lord of the imagination in his combination of wine and poetry? The thirteenth Canto collects precepts by Kung Fu (Confucius) defining 'order', to form something structurally a bit similar to a Platonic dialogue. Each Canto is composed, in its different way, of fragments carefully put together, and it might have struck a contemporary that Pound's juxtaposition of them was similar to the collagist or paste-up techniques common in the visual arts of the time.

We are not, even now, accustomed to works of verse assembled in this way; but it is important, as with any poetry to which we are new, to read with an unreasonable trust, giving ourselves to it in the act of reading aloud, thus discovering the main activity while attempting to share in it; some of the imagery will fall into place as a matter of course, while other details may be postponed as so far resistant to explanation. We understand what we can, pursuing the gist as we recreate the sound.

The rewards are already great. We read in the second Canto:

> Fish-scales over groin muscles,
> lynx-purr amid sea ...

Here, in sentence fragments, we have the transformation of the sailors into fish occurring simultaneously with the appearance of the god's big cats in the vineyard that the ship is becoming. The absence of finite verbs suggests not only the incompleteness of the images but a process going beyond human control. A wondering dreaminess of tone coincides with precision of image and language.

A good deal of the *Cantos* is concerned with economics. In 1918, Pound came across the work of Major C. H. Douglas, deviser of a scheme of monetary reform called Social Credit. Briefly, his theory arose from the belief that the value of money should be based on real goods and real work, and not on paper money or credit. Pound came to think that usury (in Latin *usura*) was the main cause of the ills of the world. The usurer, whether bank or individual money-lender, charges interest, and such interest, which is not worked for, leads to false and arbitrary values, not only in economics, but in language and art, and in fact all other aspects of our lives.

His dislike of capitalism caused Pound to be attracted to Fascism and to Mussolini himself, who was populist and anti-capitalist. And, since part of the fabric of Fascism was racism, it strengthened his dislike of Jews, associated with money-lending since the Middle Ages.

The group of Cantos directly or indirectly concerned with

usury, XLV, XLVII, and LI, dates from the 1930s, when Pound lived in Rapallo. Canto XLV, as has often been remarked, with its archaisms and its parallel clauses, its rage and its denunciations, is reminiscent of the rhetoric of the Old Testament prophet, Pound's newest persona, raving about the city's sins in the open streets.

Canto XLVII is among Pound's most remarkable works. It can be read as a self-sufficient poem, and a few careful readings aloud will make the outlines clear and leave few obscurities. If it contains fragments of Greek, we are told at once how to pronounce them, and we soon realize that they are incantatory, being exclamations of religious adoration for Adonis. Taking its starting point from the same incidents of the *Odyssey* as Canto I, this Canto concerns ancient wisdom, from Hesiod's advice about the dates of ploughing to descriptions of the votive candles placed in small jars that floated out to sea in a July festival of the Madonna, a ceremony still performed annually in Rapallo as late as 1933. We return again and again to the connections between death and fertility. 'The light has entered the cave. Io! Io!' Religious and orgasmic ecstasy are one. The god enters the cave, the plough enters the earth, the man enters the woman, Odysseus enters the porch of the underworld, we all enter the ground in our death, and in doing so make it fertile.

This Canto is grouped among the anti-usury Cantos, clearly to contrast with them. This is *real* value. Wheat at the altar, olives on the trees, semen in the womb – these are the contrast to paper money, of which the growth is *contra naturam*, against nature. Canto LI is a good deal more dense, the purpose of its juxtapositions needing to be puzzled over at greater length. The bulk of it is taken up by a contrast between a reprise of the prophetic denunciation from Canto XLV and a block of phrases from an 1828 guide to the making of artificial trout flies, exemplifying the careful craftsman who captures the rich products of the world by his creation of lures through organic materials. The difference between styles is extreme, but it is left up to us to get the gist of the contrast in the material. Other items included in this Canto are brief and sometimes obscure in allusion. The poem ends with two Chinese characters which signify 'right name' – the proper wording that is as necessary to honest discussion as it is to good poetry. Accurate language is part of the world's health, and to call something by its right name is part of true knowledge.

Pound was still in Rapallo during World War II, and made a series of eccentric propaganda broadcasts over Radio Rome to America. Since he was still a citizen of the United States, he was thus open to a charge of treason. In 1945 he was arrested by the US Army and held in an army prison camp at Pisa, where he was placed in solitary confinement in a large outdoor cage. He was later allowed the privacy of a small tent within this cage. It was in such circumstances that he awaited his removal to the United States and that he composed what are now known as the Pisan Cantos, which were not to be published for several years. After his return, he was judged mentally unfit to stand trial, and was kept in St Elizabeth's Hospital for the insane, in Washington, for almost the next thirteen years.

The Pisan Cantos were completely unforeseen, as were the conditions of their writing. By contrast to the carefully planned organization of the earlier Cantos, these formed an almost continuous unit of reflection, proceeding as a stream of consciousness (that is, by association), and for the first time consistently personal in point of view. Pound was writing in every expectation of a death sentence, and amid the ruin of his political hopes, deluded though they may have been.

> As a lone ant from a broken anthill,
> from the wreckage of Europe
> ego scriptor.

His material is partly from the daily life of the prison camp:

details about the guards and fellow prisoners, gossip about who is on sick call, notations about the birth of a wasp, the appearance of lizards or ants by or in his cage.

> When the mind swings by a grass-blade
> an ant's forefoot shall save you

by the beauty and adequacy of its mere being, a fact in the world, not in the mind. He also writes partly of the past – memories above all of his days in England before World War I, of Yeats, Maurice Hewlett, Wilfred Scawen Blunt and his wife Lady Anne. Included here is a snatch of song about the violence of sixteenth-century England, however much the Tudors had managed to reconcile the opposed roses of York and Lancaster from the Wars of the Roses. In his tent he hallucinates the eyes of a goddess, reproaching him for his faults, to whom he seeks to justify himself. It is worth noting that both these excerpts depend for much of their strength on the iambic line he had by no means abandoned when he sought out other forms of versification earlier in his career.

Pound believed that literature was news that stays news, and surely by now he has proved himself among those who continue newsworthy. He was probably the single most influential poet of the century, the generous encourager of poets from Frost to Zukofsky, the friend of Williams and Bunting, the editor of *The Waste Land*. His poetry is often difficult, but the payment for study and annotation is normally made to us in full. His politics were abhorrent, but if we forgive Hazlitt for his admiration of Napoleon then we should be prepared to do likewise to Pound for his delusions about Mussolini. And at least he apologized for his anti-Semitism at the last minute, which is more than his genteeler contemporaries did. In any case, he is demonstrably a poet of the highest order. A short selection from his poems, 'The Return', 'The Spring', *Cathay*, Propertius VI, the description of the metamorphosis on Acoetes' ship, the whole of Canto XLVII, innumerable passages from the Pisan

Cantos – these just for a start are enough to keep him among the headlines for a few centuries.

With further reading of Pound, the reader will be helped, as I have been, by the writings of Michael Alexander, Donald Davie, George Dekker, Christine Froula, Hugh Kenner, Noel Stock, and the several Guides and Companions to the *Cantos*. William Cookson has been kind with his advice.

Thom Gunn

1

Mesmerism

'And a cat's in the water-butt.' – ROBERT BROWNING

Aye you're a man that! ye old mesmerizer
Tyin' your meanin' in seventy swadelin's,
One must of needs be a hang'd early riser
To catch you at worm turning. Holy Odd's bodykins!

'Cat's i' the water butt!' Thought's in your verse-barrel,
Tell us this thing rather, then we'll believe you,
You, Master Bob Browning, spite your apparel
Jump to your sense and give praise as we'd lief do.

You wheeze as a head-cold long-tonsilled Calliope,
But God! what a sight you ha' got o' our in'ards,
Mad as a hatter but surely no Myope,
Broad as all ocean and leanin' man-kin'ards.

Heart that was big as the bowels of Vesuvius,
Words that were wing'd as her sparks in eruption,
Eagled and thundered as Jupiter Pluvius,
Sound in your wind past all signs o' corruption.

Here's to you, Old Hippety-Hop o' the accents,
True to the Truth's sake and crafty dissector,
You grabbed at the gold sure; had no need to pack cents
Into your versicles.
                              Clear sight's elector!

To Whistler, American

On the loan exhibit of his paintings at the Tate Gallery.

You also, our first great,
Had tried all ways;
Tested and pried and worked in many fashions,
And this much gives me heart to play the game.

Here is a part that's slight, and part gone wrong,
And much of little moment, and some few
Perfect as Dürer!

'In the Studio' and these two portraits, if I had my choice!
And then these sketches in the mood of Greece?

You had your searches, your uncertainties,
And this is good to know – for us, I mean,
Who bear the brunt of our America
And try to wrench her impulse into art.

You were not always sure, not always set
To hiding night or tuning 'symphonies';
Had not one style from birth, but tried and pried
And stretched and tampered with the media.

You and Abe Lincoln from that mass of dolts
Show us there's chance at least of winning through.

Sestina: Altaforte

LOQUITUR: En *Bertrans de Born.*

Dante Alighieri put this man in hell for that he was a stirrer up of strife.

Eccovi!

Judge ye!

Have I dug him up again?

The scene is at his castle, Altaforte. 'Papiols' is his jongleur.

'The Leopard,' the device *of Richard Cœur de Lion.*

I

Damn it all! all this our South stinks peace.
You whoreson dog, Papiols, come! Let's to music!
I have no life save when the swords clash.
But ah! when I see the standards gold, vair, purple, opposing
And the broad fields beneath them turn crimson,
Then howl I my heart nigh mad with rejoicing.

II

In hot summer have I great rejoicing
When the tempests kill the earth's foul peace,
And the lightnings from black heav'n flash crimson,
And the fierce thunders roar me their music
And the winds shriek through the clouds mad, opposing,
And through all the riven skies God's swords clash.

III

Hell grant soon we hear again the swords clash!
And the shrill neighs of destriers in battle rejoicing,
Spiked breast to spiked breast opposing!
Better one hour's stour than a year's peace
With fat boards, bawds, wine and frail music!
Bah! there's no wine like the blood's crimson!

IV

And I love to see the sun rise blood-crimson.
And I watch his spears through the dark clash
And it fills all my heart with rejoicing
And pries wide my mouth with fast music
When I see him so scorn and defy peace,
His lone might 'gainst all darkness opposing.

V

The man who fears war and squats opposing
My words for stour, hath no blood of crimson
But is fit only to rot in womanish peace
Far from where worth's won and the swords clash
For the death of such sluts I go rejoicing;
Yea, I fill all the air with my music.

VI

Papiols, Papiols, to the music!
There's no sound like to swords swords opposing,
No cry like the battle's rejoicing
When our elbows and swords drip the crimson
And our charges 'gainst 'The Leopard's' rush clash.
May God damn for ever all who cry 'Peace!'

VII

And let the music of the swords make them crimson!
Hell grant soon we hear again the swords clash!
Hell blot black for alway the thought 'Peace'!

Ballad of the Goodly Fere

Simon Zelotes speaketh it somewhile after the Crucifixion.
Fere = Mate, Companion.

Ha' we lost the goodliest fere o' all
For the priests and the gallows tree?
Aye lover he was of brawny men,
O' ships and the open sea.

When they came wi' a host to take Our Man
His smile was good to see,
'First let these go!' quo' our Goodly Fere,
'Or I'll see ye damned,' says he.

Aye he sent us out through the crossed high spears
And the scorn of his laugh rang free,
'Why took ye not me when I walked about
Alone in the town?' says he.

Oh we drunk his 'Hale' in the good red wine
When we last made company,
No capon priest was the Goodly Fere
But a man o' men was he.

I ha' seen him drive a hundred men
Wi' a bundle o' cords swung free,
That they took the high and holy house
For their pawn and treasury.

They'll no' get him a' in a book I think
Though they write it cunningly;
No mouse of the scrolls was the Goodly Fere
But aye loved the open sea.

If they think they ha' snared our Goodly Fere
They are fools to the last degree.
'I'll go to the feast,' quo' our Goodly Fere,
'Though I go to the gallows tree.'

'Ye ha' seen me heal the lame and blind,
And wake the dead,' says he,
'Ye shall see one thing to master all:
'Tis how a brave man dies on the tree.'

A son of God was the Goodly Fere
That bade us his brothers be.
I ha' seen him cow a thousand men.
I have seen him upon the tree.

He cried no cry when they drave the nails
And the blood gushed hot and free,
The hounds of the crimson sky gave tongue
But never a cry cried he.

I ha' seen him cow a thousand men
On the hills o' Galilee,
They whined as he walked out calm between,
Wi' his eyes like the grey o' the sea,

Like the sea that brooks no voyaging
With the winds unleashed and free,
Like the sea that he cowed at Genseret
Wi' twey words spoke' suddenly.

A master of men was the Goodly Fere,
A mate of the wind and sea,
If they think they ha' slain our Goodly Fere
They are fools eternally.

I ha' seen him eat o' the honey-comb
Sin' they nailed him to the tree.

Rome

From the French of Joachim du Bellay
'Troica Roma resurges.' – PROPERTIS

O thou new comer who seek'st Rome in Rome
And find'st in Rome no thing thou canst call Roman;
Arches worn old and palaces made common,
Rome's name alone within these walls keeps home.

Behold how pride and ruin can befall
One who hath set the whole world 'neath her laws,
All-conquering, now conquerèd, because
She is Time's prey and Time consumeth all.

Rome that art Rome's one sole last monument,
Rome that alone hast conquered Rome the town,
Tiber alone, transient and seaward bent,
Remains of Rome. O world, thou unconstant mime!
That which stands firm in thee Time batters down,
And that which fleeteth doth outrun swift time.

Portrait d'une Femme

Your mind and you are our Sargasso Sea,
London has swept about you this score years
And bright ships left you this or that in fee:
Ideas, old gossip, oddments of all things,
Strange spars of knowledge and dimmed wares of price.
Great minds have sought you – lacking someone else.
You have been second always. Tragical?
No. You preferred it to the usual thing:
One dull man, dulling and uxorious,
One average mind – with one thought less, each year.
Oh, you are patient, I have seen you sit
Hours, where something might have floated up.
And now you pay one. Yes, you richly pay.
You are a person of some interest, one comes to you
And takes strange gain away:
Trophies fished up; some curious suggestion;
Fact that leads nowhere; and a tale or two,
Pregnant with mandrakes, or with something else
That might prove useful and yet never proves,
That never fits a corner or shows use,
Or finds its hour upon the loom of days:
The tarnished, gaudy, wonderful old work;
Idols and ambergris and rare inlays,
These are your riches, your great store; and yet
For all this sea-hoard of deciduous things,
Strange woods half sodden, and new brighter stuff:
In the slow float of differing light and deep,
No! there is nothing! In the whole and all,
Nothing that's quite your own
                    Yet this is you.

The Seafarer

From the Anglo-Saxon

May I for my own self song's truth reckon,
Journey's jargon, how I in harsh days
Hardship endured oft.
Bitter breast-cares have I abided,
Known on my keel many a care's hold,
And dire sea-surge, and there I oft spent
Narrow nightwatch nigh the ship's head
While she tossed close to cliffs. Coldly afflicted,
My feet were by frost benumbed.
Chill its chains are; chafing sighs
Hew my heart round and hunger begot
Mere-weary mood. Lest man know not
That he on dry land loveliest liveth,
List how I, care-wretched, on ice-cold sea,
Weathered the winter, wretched outcast
Deprived of my kinsmen;
Hung with hard ice-flakes, where hail-scur flew,
There I heard naught save the harsh sea
And ice-cold wave, at whiles the swan cries,
Did for my games the gannet's clamour,
Sea-fowls' loudness was for me laughter,
The mews' singing all my mead-drink.
Storms, on the stone-cliffs beaten, fell on the stern
In icy feathers; full oft the eagle screamed
With spray on his pinion.
                              Not any protector
May make merry man faring needy.
This he little believes, who aye in winsome life
Abides 'mid burghers some heavy business,
Wealthy and wine-flushed, how I weary oft
Must bide above brine.
Neareth nightshade, snoweth from north,

Frost froze the land, hail fell on earth then,
Corn of the coldest. Nathless there knocketh now
The heart's thought that I on high streams
The salt-wavy tumult traverse alone.
Moaneth alway my mind's lust
That I fare forth, that I afar hence
Seek out a foreign fastness.
For this there's no mood-lofty man over earth's midst,
Not though he be given his good, but will have in his youth
   greed;
Nor his deed to the daring, nor his king to the faithful
But shall have his sorrow for sea-fare
Whatever his lord will.
He hath not heart for harping, nor in ring-having
Nor winsomeness to wife, nor world's delight
Nor any whit else save the wave's slash,
Yet longing comes upon him to fare forth on the water.
Bosque taketh blossom, cometh beauty of berries,
Fields to fairness, land fares brisker,
All this admonisheth man eager of mood,
The heart turns to travel so that he then thinks
On flood-ways to be far departing.
Cuckoo calleth with gloomy crying,
He singeth summerward, bodeth sorrow,
The bitter heart's blood. Burgher knows not –
He the prosperous man – what some perform
Where wandering them widest draweth.
So that but now my heart burst from my breastlock,
My mood 'mid the mere-flood,
Over the whale's acre, would wander wide.
On earth's shelter cometh oft to me,
Eager and ready, the crying lone-flyer,
Whets for the whale-path the heart irresistibly,
O'er tracks of ocean; seeing that anyhow
My lord deems to me this dead life
On loan and on land, I believe not

That any earth-weal eternal standeth
Save there be somewhat calamitous
That, ere a man's tide go, turn it to twain.
Disease or oldness or sword-hate
Beats out the breath from doom-gripped body.
And for this, every earl whatever, for those speaking after –
Laud of the living, boasteth some last word,
That he will work ere he pass onward,
Frame on the fair earth 'gainst foes his malice,
Daring ado, ...
So that all men shall honour him after
And his laud beyond them remain 'mid the English,
Aye, for ever, a lasting life's-blast,
Delight 'mid the doughty.
                                        Days little durable,
And all arrogance of earthen riches,
There come now no kings nor Cæsars
Nor gold-giving lords like those gone.
Howe'er in mirth most magnified,
Whoe'er lived in life most lordliest,
Drear all this excellence, delights undurable!
Waneth the watch, but the world holdeth.
Tomb hideth trouble. The blade is layed low.
Earthly glory ageth and seareth.
No man at all going the earth's gait,
But age fares against him, his face paleth,
Grey-haired he groaneth, knows gone companions,
Lordly men, are to earth o'ergiven,
Nor may he then the flesh-cover, whose life ceaseth,
Nor eat the sweet nor feel the sorry,
Nor stir hand nor think in mid heart,
And though he strew the grave with gold,
His born brothers, their buried bodies
Be an unlikely treasure hoard.

The Return

See, they return; ah, see the tentative
    Movements, and the slow feet,
    The trouble in the pace and the uncertain
    Wavering!

See, they return, one, and by one,
With fear, as half-awakened;
As if the snow should hesitate
And murmur in the wind,
            and half turn back;
These were the 'Wing'd-with-Awe,'
            Inviolable.

Gods of the wingèd shoe!
With them the silver hounds,
            sniffing the trace of air!

Haie! Haie!
    These were the swift to harry;
These the keen-scented;
These were the souls of blood.

Slow on the leash,
            pallid the leash-men!

[epigraph to *Lustra*]

And the days are not full enough
And the nights are not full enough
And life slips by like a field mouse
        Not shaking the grass.

The Garret

Come, let us pity those who are better off than we are.
Come, my friend, and remember
        that the rich have butlers and no friends,
And we have friends and no butlers.
Come, let us pity the married and the unmarried.

Dawn enters with little feet
        like a gilded Pavlova,
And I am near my desire.
Nor has life in it aught better
Than this hour of clear coolness,
        the hour of waking together.

The Garden

En robe de parade. – SAMAIN

Like a skein of loose silk blown against a wall
She walks by the railing of a path in Kensington Gardens,
And she is dying piece-meal
      of a sort of emotional anæmia.

And round about there is a rabble
Of the filthy, sturdy, unkillable infants of the very poor.
They shall inherit the earth.

In her is the end of breeding.
Her boredom is exquisite and excessive.
She would like some one to speak to her,
And is almost afraid that I
      will commit that indiscretion.

The Spring

'Ηρι μεν άί τε κυδώνιαι – IBYCUS

Cydonian Spring with her attendant train,
Maelids and water-girls,
Stepping beneath a boisterous wind from Thrace,
Throughout this sylvan place
Spreads the bright tips,
And every vine-stock is
Clad in new brilliancies.
                              And wild desire
Falls like black lightning.
O bewildered heart,
Though every branch have back what last year lost,
She, who moved here amid the cyclamen,
Moves only now a clinging tenuous ghost.

April

Nympharum membra disjecta

Three spirits came to me
And drew me apart
To where the olive boughs
Lay stripped upon the ground:
Pale carnage beneath bright mist.

Les Millwin

The little Millwins attend the Russian Ballet.
The mauve and greenish souls of the little Millwins
Were seen lying along the upper seats
Like so many unused boas.

The turbulent and undisciplined host of art students –
The rigorous deputation from 'Slade' –
Was before them.

With arms exalted, with fore-arms
Crossed in great futuristic X's, the art students
Exulted, they beheld the splendours of *Cleopatra*.

And the little Millwins beheld these things;
With their large and anæmic eyes they looked out upon this
    configuration.

Let us therefore mention the fact,
For it seems to us worthy of record.

The Study in Aesthetics

The very small children in patched clothing,
Being smitten with an unusual wisdom,
Stopped in their play as she passed them
And cried up from their cobbles:

>   *Guarda! Ahi, guarda! ch' è be'a!*[1]

But three years after this
I heard the young Dante, whose last name I do not know –
For there are, in Sirmione, twenty-eight young Dantes and
    thirty-four Catulli;
And there had been a great catch of sardines,
And his elders
Were packing them in the great wooden boxes
For the market in Brescia, and he
Leapt about, snatching at the bright fish
And getting in both of their ways;
And in vain they commanded him to *sta fermo!*
And when they would not let him arrange
The fish in the boxes
He stroked those which were already arranged,
Murmuring for his own satisfaction
This identical phrase:

>   *Ch' è be'a.*

And at this I was mildly abashed.

1. Bella

Liu Ch'e

The rustling of the silk is discontinued,
Dust drifts over the court-yard,
There is no sound of foot-fall, and the leaves
Scurry into heaps and lie still,
And she the rejoicer of the heart is beneath them:

A wet leaf that clings to the threshold.

In a Station of the Metro

The apparition   of these faces   in the crowd   :
Petals   on a wet, black   bough   .

   [First version: *Poetry*, 1913]

Alba

As cool as the pale wet leaves
                      of lily-of-the-valley
She lay beside me in the dawn.

Coitus

The gilded phaloi of the crocuses
               are thrusting at the spring air.
Here is there naught of dead gods
But a procession of festival,
A procession, O Giulio Romano,
Fit for your spirit to dwell in.
Dione, your nights are upon us.

The dew is upon the leaf.
The night about us is restless.

Society

The family position was waning,
And on this account the little Aurelia,
Who had laughed on eighteen summers,
Now bears the palsied contact of Phidippus.

The Gypsy

'Est-ce que vous avez vu des autres – des
camarades – avec des singes ou des ours?'
A STRAY GIPSY, AD 1912

That was the top of the walk, when he said:
'Have you seen any others, any of our lot,
With apes or bears?'
       – A brown upstanding fellow
Not like the half-castes,
       up on the wet road near Clermont.
The wind came, and the rain,
And mist clotted about the trees in the valley,
And I'd the long ways behind me,
       gray Arles and Biaucaire,
And he said, 'Have you seen any of our lot?'
I'd seen a lot of his lot . . .
       ever since Rhodez,
Coming down from the fair
       of St John,
With caravans, but never an ape or a bear.

Alba

(from 'Langue d'Oc')

When the nightingale to his mate
Sings day-long and night late
My love and I keep state
In bower,
In flower,
'Till the watchman on the tower
Cry:
       'Up! Thou rascal, Rise,
       I see the white
          Light
          And the night
             Flies.'

2 *from* Cathay

For the most part from the Chinese of Rihaku [Li Po], from the notes of the late Ernest Fenollosa, and the decipherings of the professors Mori and Ariga

Song of the Bowmen of Shu

Here we are, picking the first fern-shoots
And saying: When shall we get back to our country?
Here we are because we have the Ken-nin for our foemen,
We have no comfort because of these Mongols.
We grub the soft fern-shoots,
When anyone says 'Return,' the others are full of sorrow.
Sorrowful minds, sorrow is strong, we are hungry and
    thirsty.
Our defence is not yet made sure, no one can let his friend
    return.
We grub the old fern-stalks.
We say: Will we be let to go back in October?
There is no ease in royal affairs, we have no comfort.
Our sorrow is bitter, but we would not return to our country.
What flower has come into blossom?
Whose chariot? The General's.
Horses, his horses even, are tired. They were strong.
We have no rest, three battles a month.
By heaven, his horses are tired.
The generals are on them, the soldiers are by them.
The horses are well trained, the generals have ivory arrows
    and quivers ornamented with fish-skin.
The enemy is swift, we must be careful.
When we set out, the willows were drooping with spring,
We come back in the snow,
We go slowly, we are hungry and thirsty,
Our mind is full of sorrow, who will know of our grief?

By Bunno, reputedly 1100 BC

The Beautiful Toilet

Blue, blue is the grass about the river
And the willows have overfilled the close garden.
And within, the mistress, in the midmost of her youth,
White, white of face, hesitates, passing the door.
Slender, she puts forth a slender hand;

And she was a courtezan in the old days,
And she has married a sot,
Who now goes drunkenly out
And leaves her too much alone.

By Mei Sheng, 140 BC

The River Song

This boat is of shato-wood, and its gunwales are cut
    magnolia,
Musicians with jewelled flutes and with pipes of gold
Fill full the sides in rows, and our wine
Is rich for a thousand cups.
We carry singing girls, drift with the drifting water,
Yet Sennin needs
A yellow stork for a charger, and all our seamen
Would follow the white gulls or ride them.
Kutsu's prose song
Hangs with the sun and moon.

King So's terraced palace
                is now but barren hill,
But I draw pen on this barge
Causing the five peaks to tremble,
And I have joy in these words
                like the joy of blue islands.
(If glory could last forever
Then the waters of Han would flow northward.)
        *

And I have moped in the Emperor's garden, awaiting an
    order-to-write!
I looked at the dragon-pond, with its willow-coloured water
Just reflecting the sky's tinge,
And heard the five-score nightingales aimlessly singing.

The eastern wind brings the green colour into the island
    grasses at Yei-shu,
The purple house and the crimson are full of Spring softness.
South of the pond the willow-tips are half-blue and bluer,
Their cords tangle in mist, against the brocade-like palace.
Vine-strings a hundred feet long hang down from carved
    railings,

And high over the willows, the fine birds sing to each other,
and listen,
Crying – 'Kwan, Kuan,' for the early wind, and the feel of it.
The wind bundles itself into a bluish cloud and wanders off.
Over a thousand gates, over a thousand doors are the sounds
of spring singing,
And the Emperor is at Ko.
Five clouds hang aloft, bright on the purple sky,
The imperial guards come forth from the golden house with
their armour a-gleaming.
The Emperor in his jewelled car goes out to inspect his
flowers,
He goes out to Hori, to look at the wing-flapping storks,
He returns by way of Sei rock, to hear the new nightingales,
For the gardens at Jo-run are full of new nightingales,
Their sound is mixed in this flute,
Their voice is in the twelve pipes here.

By Rihaku, 8th century AD

The River-Merchant's Wife: A Letter

While my hair was still cut straight across my forehead
I played about the front gate, pulling flowers.
You came by on bamboo stilts, playing horse,
You walked about my seat, playing with blue plums.
And we went on living in the village of Chokan:
Two small people, without dislike or suspicion.

At fourteen I married My Lord you.
I never laughed, being bashful.
Lowering my head, I looked at the wall.
Called to, a thousand times, I never looked back.

At fifteen I stopped scowling,
I desired my dust to be mingled with yours
Forever and forever and forever.
Why should I climb the look out?

At sixteen you departed,
You went into far Ku-to-yen, by the river of swirling eddies,
And you have been gone five months.
The monkeys make sorrowful noise overhead.
You dragged your feet when you went out.
By the gate now, the moss is grown, the different mosses,
Too deep to clear them away!
The leaves fall early this autumn, in wind.
The paired butterflies are already yellow with August
Over the grass in the West garden;
They hurt me. I grow older.
If you are coming down through the narrows of the river
    Kiang,
Please let me know beforehand,
And I will come out to meet you
                As far as Cho-fu-Sa.

By Rihaku

Poem by the Bridge at Ten-Shin

March has come to the bridge head,
Peach boughs and apricot boughs hang over a thousand
   gates,
At morning there are flowers to cut the heart,
And evening drives them on the eastward-flowing waters.
Petals are on the gone waters and on the going,
       And on the back-swirling eddies,
But to-day's men are not the men of the old days,
Though they hang in the same way over the bridge-rail.

The sea's colour moves at the dawn
And the princes still stand in rows, about the throne,
And the moon falls over the portals of Sei-go-yo,
And clings to the walls and the gate-top.
With head gear glittering against the cloud and sun,
The lords go forth from the court, and into far borders.
They ride upon dragon-like horses,
Upon horses with head-trappings of yellow metal,
And the streets make way for their passage.
       Haughty their passing,
Haughty their steps as they go in to great banquets,
To high halls and curious food,
To the perfumed air and girls dancing,
To clear flutes and clear singing;
To the dance of the seventy couples;
To the mad chase through the gardens.
Night and day are given over to pleasure
And they think it will last a thousand autumns,
       Unwearying autumns.
For them the yellow dogs howl portents in vain,
And what are they compared to the lady Riokushu,
       That was cause of hate!
Who among them is a man like Han-rei

Who departed alone with his mistress,
With her hair unbound, and he his own skiffsman!

By Rihaku

The Jewel Stairs' Grievance

The jewelled steps are already quite white with dew,
It is so late that the dew soaks my gauze stockings,
And I let down the crystal curtain
And watch the moon through the clear autumn.

By Rihaku

NOTE – Jewel stairs, therefore a palace. Grievance, therefore there is
something to complain of. Gauze stockings, therefore a court lady,
not a servant who complains. Clear autumn, therefore he has no
excuse on account of weather. Also she has come early, for the dew
has not merely whitened the stairs, but has soaked her stockings. The
poem is especially prized because she utters no direct reproach.

Lament of the Frontier Guard

By the North Gate, the wind blows full of sand,
Lonely from the beginning of time until now!
Trees fall, the grass goes yellow with autumn.
I climb the towers and towers
        to watch out the barbarous land:
Desolate castle, the sky, the wide desert.
There is no wall left to this village.
Bones white with a thousand frosts,
High heaps, covered with trees and grass;
Who brought this to pass?
Who has brought the flaming imperial anger?
Who has brought the army with drums and with kettle-
    drums?
Barbarous kings.
A gracious spring, turned to blood-ravenous autumn,
A turmoil of wars-men, spread over the middle kingdom,
Three hundred and sixty thousand,
And sorrow, sorrow like rain.
Sorrow to go, and sorrow, sorrow returning.
Desolate, desolate fields,
And no children of warfare upon them,
        No longer the men for offence and defence.
Ah, how shall you know the dreary sorrow at the North Gate,
With Riboku's name forgotten,
And we guardsmen fed to the tigers.

    By Rihaku

Exile's Letter

To So-Kin of Rakuyo, ancient friend, Chancellor of Gen.
Now I remember that you built me a special tavern
By the south side of the bridge at Ten-Shin.
With yellow gold and white jewels, we paid for songs and
    laughter
And we were drunk for month on month, forgetting the
    kings and princes.
Intelligent men came drifting in from the sea and from the
    west border,
And with them, and with you especially
There was nothing at cross purpose,
And they made nothing of sea-crossing or of mountain-
    crossing,
If only they could be of that fellowship,
And we all spoke out our hearts and minds, and without
    regret.
And then I was sent off to South Wei,
            smothered in laurel groves,
And you to the north of Raku-hoku,
Till we had nothing but thoughts and memories in common.
And then, when separation had come to its worst,
We met, and travelled into Sen-Go,
Through all the thirty-six folds of the turning and twisting
    waters,
Into a valley of the thousand bright flowers,
That was the first valley;
And into ten thousand valleys full of voices and pine-winds.
And with silver harness and reins of gold,
Out came the East of Kan foreman and his company.
And there came also the 'True man' of Shi-yo to meet me,
Playing on a jewelled mouth-organ.
In the storied houses of San-Ko they gave us more Sennin
    music,

40

Many instruments, like the sound of young phœnix broods.
The foreman of Kan Chu, drunk, danced
        because his long sleeves wouldn't keep still
With that music playing,
And I, wrapped in brocade, went to sleep with my head on
    his lap,
And my spirit so high it was all over the heavens,
And before the end of the day we were scattered like stars, or
    rain.
I had to be off to So, far away over the waters,
You back to your river-bridge.

And your father, who was brave as a leopard,
Was governor in Hei Shu, and put down the barbarian
    rabble.
And one May he had you send for me,
        despite the long distance.
And what with broken wheels and so on, I won't say it wasn't
    hard going,
Over roads twisted like sheep's guts.
And I was still going, late in the year,
        in the cutting wind from the North,
And thinking how little you cared for the cost,
        and you caring enough to pay it.
And what a reception:
Red jade cups, food well set on a blue jewelled table,
And I was drunk, and had no thought of returning.
And you would walk out with me to the western corner of
    the castle,
To the dynastic temple, with water about it clear as blue jade,
With boats floating, and the sound of mouth-organs and
    drums,
With ripples like dragon-scales, going grass green on the
    water,
Pleasure lasting, with courtezans, going and coming without
    hindrance,

With the willow flakes falling like snow,
And the vermilioned girls getting drunk about sunset,
And the water, a hundred feet deep, reflecting green
    eyebrows
– Eyebrows painted green are a fine sight in young
    moonlight,
Gracefully painted –
And the girls singing back at each other,
Dancing in transparent brocade,
And the wind lifting the song, and interrupting it,
Tossing it up under the clouds.
        And all this comes to an end.
        And is not again to be met with.
I went up to the court for examination,
Tried Layu's luck, offered the Choyo song,
And got no promotion,
        and went back to the East Mountains
        White-headed.
And once again, later, we met at the South bridge-head.
And then the crowd broke up, you went north to San palace,
And if you ask how I regret that parting:
It is like the flowers falling at Spring's end
        Confused, whirled in a tangle.
What is the use of talking, and there is no end of talking,
There is no end of things in the heart.
I call in the boy,
Have him sit on his knees here
        To seal this,
And send it a thousand miles, thinking.

    By Rihaku

Taking Leave of a Friend

Blue mountains to the north of the walls,
White river winding about them;
Here we must make separation
And go out through a thousand miles of dead grass.

Mind like a floating wide cloud,
Sunset like the parting of old acquaintances
Who bow over their clasped hands at a distance.
Our horses neigh to each other
        as we are departing.

   Rihaku

Sennin Poem by Kakuhaku

The red and green kingfishers
        flash between the orchids and clover,
One bird casts its gleam on another.

Green vines hang through the high forest,
They weave a whole roof to the mountain,
The lone man sits with shut speech,
He purrs and pats the clear strings.
He throws his heart up through the sky,
He bites through the flower pistil
        and brings up a fine fountain.

The red-pine-tree god looks at him and wonders.
He rides through the purple smoke to visit the sennin,
He takes 'Floating Hill' by the sleeve,
He claps his hand on the back of the great water sennin.

But you, you dam'd crowd of gnats,
Can you even tell the age of a turtle?

A Ballad of the Mulberry Road

The sun rises in south east corner of things
To look on the tall house of the Shin
For they have a daughter named Rafu,
      (pretty girl)
She made the name for herself: 'Gauze Veil,'
For she feeds mulberries to silkworms.
She gets them by the south wall of the town.
With green strings she makes the warp of her basket,
She makes the shoulder-straps of her basket
      from the boughs of Katsura,
And she piles her hair up on the left side of her head-piece.

Her earrings are made of pearl,
Her underskirt is of green pattern-silk,
Her overskirt is the same silk dyed in purple,
And when men going by look on Rafu
      They set down their burdens,
They stand and twirl their moustaches.

   (Fenollosa Mss, very early)

Old Idea of Choan by Rosoriu

I

The narrow streets cut into the wide highway at Choan,
Dark oxen, white horses,
       drag on the seven coaches with outriders.
The coaches are perfumed wood,
The jewelled chair is held up at the crossway,
Before the royal lodge:
A glitter of golden saddles, awaiting the princess;
They eddy before the gate of the barons.
The canopy embroidered with dragons
       drinks in and casts back the sun.
Evening comes.
       The trappings are bordered with mist.
The hundred cords of mist are spread through
       and double the trees,
Night birds, and night women,
Spread out their sounds through the gardens.

II

Birds with flowery wing, hovering butterflies
       crowd over the thousand gates,
Trees that glitter like jade,
       terraces tinged with silver,
The seed of a myriad hues,
A net-work of arbours and passages and covered ways,
Double towers, winged roofs,
       border the net-work of ways:
A place of felicitous meeting.
Riu's house stands out on the sky,
       with glitter of colour
As Butei of Kan had made the high golden lotus
       to gather his dews,

Before it another house which I do not know:
How shall we know all the friends
whom we meet on strange roadways?

To-Em-Mei's 'The Unmoving Cloud'

'Wet springtime,' says To-Em-Mei,
'Wet spring in the garden.'

I

The clouds have gathered, and gathered,
        and the rain falls and falls,
The eight ply of the heavens
        are all folded into one darkness,
And the wide, flat road stretches out.
I stop in my room toward the East, quiet, quiet,
I pat my new cask of wine.
My friends are estranged, or far distant,
I bow my head and stand still.

II

Rain, rain, and the clouds have gathered,
The eight ply of the heavens are darkness,
The flat land is turned into river.
        'Wine, wine, here is wine!'
I drink by my eastern window.
I think of talking and man,
And no boat, no carriage, approaches.

III

The trees in my east-looking garden
        are bursting out with new twigs,
They try to stir new affection,
And men say the sun and moon keep on moving
        because they can't find a soft seat.
The birds flutter to rest in my tree,
        and I think I have heard them saying,

'It is not that there are no other men
But we like this fellow the best,
But however we long to speak
He can not know of our sorrow.'

T'ao Yuan Ming, AD 365–427

3 *from* Homage to Sextus Propertius

Orfeo
   '*Quia pauper amavi.*'

I

Shades of Callimachus, Coan ghosts of Philetas
It is in your grove I would walk,
I who come first from the clear font
Bringing the Grecian orgies into Italy,
                    and the dance into Italy.
Who hath taught you so subtle a measure,
               in what hall have you heard it;
What foot beat out your time-bar,
          what water has mellowed your whistles?

Out-weariers of Apollo will, as we know, continue their
   Martian generalities,
   We have kept our erasers in order.
A new-fangled chariot follows the flower-hung horses;
A young Muse with loves clustered about her
               ascends with me into the æther, ...
And there is no high-road to the Muses.

Annalists will continue to record Roman reputations,
Celebrities from the Trans-Caucasus will belaud Roman
   celebrities
And expound the distentions of Empire,
But for something to read in normal circumstances?
For a few pages brought down from the forked hill unsullied?
I ask a wreath which will not crush my head.
               And there is no hurry about it;
I shall have, doubtless, a boom after my funeral,
Seeing that long standing increases all things
                  regardless of quality.
And who would have known the towers
             pulled down by a deal-wood horse;
Or of Achilles withstaying waters by Simois
Or of Hector spattering wheel-rims,

Or of Polydmantus, by Scamander, or Helenus and
    Deiphoibos?
Their door-yards would scarcely know them, or Paris.
Small talk O Ilion, and O Troad
                            twice taken by Oetian gods,
If Homer had not stated your case!

And I also among the later nephews of this city
                            shall have my dog's day,
With no stone upon my contemptible sepulchre;
My vote coming from the temple of Phoebus in Lycia, at
    Patara,
And in the mean time my songs will travel,
And the devirginated young ladies will enjoy them
            when they have got over the strangeness,
For Orpheus tamed the wild beasts –
                        and held up the Threician river;
And Cithaeron shook up the rocks by Thebes
        and danced them into a bulwark at his pleasure,
And you, O Polyphemus? Did harsh Galatea almost
Turn to your dripping horses, because of a tune, under Aetna?
We must look into the matter.
Bacchus and Apollo in favour of it,
There will be a crowd of young women doing homage to my
    palaver,
Though my house is not propped up by Taenarian columns
    from Laconia (associated with Neptune and Cerberus),
Though it is not stretched upon gilded beams:
My orchards do not lie level and wide
                        as the forests of Phaeacia,
                        the luxurious and Ionian,
Nor are my caverns stuffed stiff with a Marcian vintage,
My cellar does not date from Numa Pompilius,
Nor bristle with wine jars,
Nor is it equipped with a frigidaire patent;

54

Yet the companions of the Muses
        will keep their collective nose in my books,
And weary with historical data, they will turn to my
    dance tune.

Happy who are mentioned in my pamphlets,
        the songs shall be a fine tomb-stone over their beauty.
            But against this?
Neither expensive pyramids scraping the stars in their route,
Nor houses modelled upon that of Jove in East Elis,
Nor the monumental effigies of Mausolus,
                    are a complete elucidation of death.

Flame burns, rain sinks into the cracks
And they all go to rack ruin beneath the thud of the years.
Stands genius a deathless adornment,
        a name not to be worn out with the years.

III

Midnight, and a letter comes to me from our mistress:
    Telling me to come to Tibur:
                        At once!!
'Bright tips reach up from twin towers,
Anienan spring water falls into flat-spread pools.'

What *is* to be done about it?
    Shall I entrust myself to entangled shadows,
Where bold hands may do violence to my person?

Yet if I postpone my obedience
                because of this respectable terror,
I shall be prey to lamentations worse than a nocturnal
    assailant.
And I shall be in the wrong,
              and it will last a twelve month,
For her hands have no kindness me-ward,

Nor is there anyone to whom lovers are not sacred at
    midnight
    And in the Via Sciro.
If any man would be a lover
             he may walk on the Scythian coast,
No barbarism would go to the extent of doing him harm,
The moon will carry his candle,
             the stars will point out the stumbles,
Cupid will carry lighted torches before him
               and keep mad dogs off his ankles.
Thus all roads are perfectly safe
               and at any hour;
Who so indecorous as to shed the pure gore of a suitor?!
    Cypris is his cicerone.
What if undertakers follow my track,
             such a death is worth dying.

She would bring frankincense and wreaths to my tomb,
    She would sit like an ornament on my pyre.

Gods' aid, let not my bones lie in a public location
With crowds too assiduous in their crossing of it;
For thus are tombs of lovers most desecrated.

May a woody and sequestered place cover me with its foliage
Or may I inter beneath the hummock
                of some as yet uncatalogued sand;
At any rate I shall not have my epitaph in a high road.

IV
Difference of Opinion With Lygdamus

Tell me the truths which you hear of our constant young
    lady,
                Lygdamus,
And may the bought yoke of a mistress lie with
                    equitable weight on your shoulders;
For I am swelled up with inane pleasurabilities
                   and deceived by your reference
To things which you think I would like to believe.

No messenger should come wholly empty,
               and a slave should fear plausibilities;
Much conversation is as good as having a home.
   Out with it, tell it to me, all of it, from the beginning,
I guzzle with outstretched ears.
Thus? She wept into uncombed hair,
                    And you saw it.
Vast waters flowed from her eyes?
                You, you Lygdamus
Saw her stretched on her bed, –
             it was no glimpse in a mirror;
No gawds on her snowy hands, no orfevrerie,
Sad garment draped on her slender arms.
Her escritoires lay shut by the bed-feet.
Sadness hung over the house, and the desolated female
    attendants
Were desolated because she had told them her dreams.

She was veiled in the midst of that place,
Damp woolly handkerchiefs were stuffed into her undryable
   eyes,
And a querulous noise responded to our solicitous
    reprobations.

For which things you will get a reward from me,
                    Lygdamus?
To say many things is equal to having a home.
And the other woman 'has not enticed me
                              by her pretty manners,
She has caught me with herbaceous poison,
            she twiddles the spiked wheel of a rhombus,
She stews puffed frogs, snake's bones, the moulted feathers
    of screech owls,

She binds me with ravvles of shrouds.
                    Black spiders spin in her bed!
Let her lovers snore at her in the morning!
                    May the gout cramp up her feet!
Does he like me to sleep here alone,
            Lygdamus?
Will he say nasty things at my funeral?'

And you expect me to believe this
                    after twelve months of discomfort?

VI

When, when, and whenever death closes our eyelids,
Moving naked over Acheron
Upon the one raft, victor and conquered together,
Marius and Jugurtha together,
                            one tangle of shadows.

Caesar plots against India,
Tigris and Euphrates shall, from now on, flow at his bidding,
Tibet shall be full of Roman policemen,
The Parthians shall get used to our statuary
                            and acquire a Roman religion;
One raft on the veiled flood of Acheron,
                    Marius and Jugurtha together.

Nor at my funeral either will there be any long trail,
                    bearing ancestral lares and images;
No trumpets filled with my emptiness,
Nor shall it be on an Atalic bed;
            The perfumed cloths shall be absent.
A small plebeian procession.
            Enough, enough and in plenty
There will be three books at my obsequies
Which I take, my not unworthy gift, to Persephone.

You will follow the bare scarified breast
Nor will you be weary of calling my name, nor too weary
            To place the last kiss on my lips
When the Syrian onyx is broken.

            'He who is now vacant dust
                Was once the slave of one passion:'
Give that much inscription
                'Death why tardily come?'

You, sometimes, will lament a lost friend,
        For it is a custom:
This care for past men,

Since Adonis was gored in Idalia, and the Cytharean
Ran crying with out-spread hair,
        In vain, you call back the shade,
In vain, Cynthia. Vain call to unanswering shadow,
        Small talk comes from small bones.

IX

1

The twisted rhombs ceased their clamour of
    accompaniment;
The scorched laurel lay in the fire-dust;
The moon still declined to descend out of heaven,

But the black ominous owl hoot was audible.

And one raft bears our fates
                on the veiled lake toward Avernus
Sails spread on Cerulean waters, I would shed tears
        for two;
I shall live, if she continue in life,
        If she dies, I shall go with her.
Great Zeus, save the woman,
          or she will sit before your feet in a veil,
          and tell out the long list of her troubles.

2

Persephone and Dis, Dis, have mercy upon her,
There are enough women in hell,
                quite enough beautiful women,
Iope, and Tyro, and Pasiphae, and the formal girls of Achaia,
And out of Troad, and from the Campania,
Death has his tooth in the lot,
            Avernus lusts for the lot of them,
Beauty is not eternal, no man has perennial fortune,
Slow foot, or swift foot, death delays but for a season.

3

My light, light of my eyes,
                you are escaped from great peril,
Go back to Great Dian's dances bearing suitable gifts,
Pay up your vow of night watches
                      to Dian goddess of virgins,
And unto me also pay debt:
The ten nights of your company you have
                    promised me.

X

Light, light of my eyes, at an exceeding late hour I was
    wandering,
And intoxicated,
                and no servant was leading me,
And a minute crowd of small boys came from opposite,
                        I do not know what boys,
And I am afraid of numerical estimate,
And some of them shook little torches,
                    and others held onto arrows,
And the rest laid their chains upon me,
            and they were naked, the lot of them,
And one of the lot was given to lust.

'That incensed female has consigned him to our pleasure.'
So spoke. And the noose was over my neck.
And another said 'Get him plumb in the middle!
        Shove along there, shove along!'
And another broke in upon this:
                'He thinks that we are not gods.'
'And she has been waiting for the scoundrel,
                and in a new Sidonian night cap,
And with more than Arabian odours,
                God knows where he has been.
She could scarcely keep her eyes open
                    enter that much for his bail.
                        Get along now!'

We were coming near to the house,
                    and they gave another yank to my cloak,
And it was morning, and I wanted to see if she was alone, and
        resting,
And Cynthia was alone in her bed.
                                    I was stupefied.
I had never seen her looking so beautiful,
            No, not when she was tunick'd in purple.

Such aspect was presented to me, me recently emerged from
        my visions,
You will observe that pure form has its value.

'You are a very early inspector of mistresses.
Do you think I have adopted your habits?'
            There were upon the bed no signs of a voluptuous
                    encounter,
                No signs of a second incumbent.

She continued:
            'No incubus has crushed his body against me,
            Though spirits are celebrated for adultery.
            And I am going to the temple of Vesta . . .'
                                        and so on.

Since that day I have had no pleasant nights.

XII

Who, who will be the next man to entrust his girl to a friend?
Love interferes with fidelities;
The gods have brought shame on their relatives;
Each man wants the pomegranate for himself;
Amiable and harmonious people are pushed incontinent
    into duels,
A Trojan and adulterous person came to Menelaus under the
    rites of hospitium,
And there was a case in Colchis, Jason and that woman in
    Colchis;
And besides, Lynceus,
                you were drunk.

Could you endure such promiscuity?
                She was not renowned for fidelity;
But to jab a knife in my vitals, to have passed on a swig of
    poison,
Preferable, my dear boy, my dear Lynceus,
Comrade, comrade of my life, of my purse, of my person;
But in one bed, in one bed alone, my dear Lynceus,
        I deprecate your attendance;
I would ask a like boon of Jove.

And you write of Achelöus, who contended with Hercules,
You write of Adrastus' horses and the funeral rites of
    Achenor,
And you will not leave off imitating Aeschylus.
        Though you make a hash of Antimachus,
You think you are going to do Homer.
        And still a girl scorns the gods,
Of all these young women
    not one has enquired the cause of the world,
Nor the modus of lunar eclipses
        Nor whether there be any patch left of us

After we cross the infernal ripples,
    nor if the thunder fall from predestination;
Nor anything else of importance.

Upon the Actian marshes Virgil is Phoebus' chief of police,
        He can tabulate Caesar's great ships.
He thrills to Ilian arms,
        He shakes the Trojan weapons of Aeneas,
And casts stores on Lavinian beaches.
Make way, ye Roman authors,
                    clear the street, O ye Greeks,
For a much larger Iliad is in the course of construction
(and to Imperial order)
Clear the streets, O ye Greeks!

And you also follow him 'neath Phrygian pine shade:
        Thyrsis and Daphnis upon whittled reeds,
And how ten sins can corrupt young maidens;
        Kids for a bribe and pressed udders,
Happy selling poor loves for cheap apples.

Tityrus might have sung the same vixen;
        Corydon tempted Alexis,
Head farmers do likewise, and lying weary amid their oats
They get praise from tolerant Hamadryads.
Go on, to Ascraeus' prescription, the ancient,
                        respected, Wordsworthian:
'A flat field for rushes, grapes grow on the slope.'

And behold me, small fortune left in my house.
Me, who had no general for a grandfather!
I shall triumph among young ladies of indeterminate
    character,
My talent acclaimed in their banquets,
        I shall be honoured with yesterday's wreaths.
And the god strikes to the marrow.

Like a trained and performing tortoise,
I would make verse in your fashion, if she should command
    it,
With her husband asking a remission of sentence,
            And even this infamy would not attract
                numerous readers
Were there an erudite or violent passion,
For the nobleness of the populace brooks nothing below its
    own altitude.
One must have resonance, resonance and sonority ... like a
    goose.

Varro sang Jason's expedition,
            Varro, of his great passion Leucadia,
There is song in the parchment; Catullus the highly
    indecorous,
Of Lesbia, known above Helen;
And in the dyed pages of Calvus,
            Calvus mourning Quintilia,
And but now Gallus had sung of Lycoris.
        Fair, fairest Lycoris –
The waters of Styx poured over the wound:
And now Propertius of Cynthia, taking his stand among
    these.

4 from *The Cantos*

Canto I

And then went down to the ship,
Set keel to breakers, forth on the godly sea, and
We set up mast and sail on that swart ship,
Bore sheep aboard her, and our bodies also
Heavy with weeping, so winds from sternward
Bore us out onward with bellying canvas,
Circe's this craft, the trim-coifed goddess.
Then sat we amidships, wind jamming the tiller,
Thus with stretched sail, we went over sea till day's end.
Sun to his slumber, shadows o'er all the ocean,
Came we then to the bounds of deepest water,
To the Kimmerian lands, and peopled cities
Covered with close-webbed mist, unpiercèd ever
With glitter of sun-rays
Nor with stars stretched, nor looking back from heaven
Swartest night stretched over wretched men there.
The ocean flowing backward, came we then to the place
Aforesaid by Circe.
Here did they rites, Perimedes and Eurylochus,
And drawing sword from my hip
I dug the ell-square pitkin;
Poured we libations unto each the dead,
First mead and then sweet wine, water mixed with white
    flour.
Then prayed I many a prayer to the sickly death's-heads;
As set in Ithaca, sterile bulls of the best
For sacrifice, heaping the pyre with goods,
A sheep to Tiresias only, black and a bell-sheep.
Dark blood flowed in the fosse,
Souls out of Erebus, cadaverous dead, of brides,
Of youths and of the old who had borne much;
Souls stained with recent tears, girls tender,
Men many, mauled with bronze lance heads,

Battle spoil, bearing yet dreory arms,
These many crowded about me; with shouting,
Pallor upon me, cried to my men for more beasts;
Slaughtered the herds, sheep slain of bronze;
Poured ointment, cried to the gods,
To Pluto the strong, and praised Proserpine;
Unsheathed the narrow sword,
I sat to keep off the impetuous impotent dead,
Till I should hear Tiresias.
But first Elpenor came, our friend Elpenor,
Unburied, cast on the wide earth,
Limbs that we left in the house of Circe,
Unwept, unwrapped in sepulchre, since toils urged other.
Pitiful spirit. And I cried in hurried speech:
'Elpenor, how art thou come to this dark coast?
Cam'st thou afoot, outstripping seamen?'
          And he in heavy speech:
'Ill fate and abundant wine. I slept in Circe's ingle.
Going down the long ladder unguarded,
I fell against the buttress,
Shattered the nape-nerve, the soul sought Avernus.
But thou, O King, I bid remember me, unwept, unburied,
Heap up mine arms, be tomb by sea-bord, and inscribed:
A man of no fortune, and with a name to come.
And set my oar up, that I swung mid fellows.'

And Anticlea came, whom I beat off, and then Tiresias
     Theban,
Holding his golden wand, knew me, and spoke first:
'A second time? why? man of ill star,
Facing the sunless dead and this joyless region?
Stand from the fosse, leave me my bloody bever
For soothsay.'
          And I stepped back,
And he strong with the blood, said then: 'Odysseus
Shalt return through spiteful Neptune, over dark seas,

Lose all companions.' Then Anticlea came.
Lie quiet Divus. I mean, that is Andreas Divus,
In officina Wecheli, 1538, out of Homer.
And he sailed, by Sirens and thence outward and away
And unto Circe.
                    Venerandam,
In the Cretan's phrase, with the golden crown, Aphrodite,
Cypri munimenta sortita est, mirthful, oricalchi, with golden
Girdles and breast bands, thou with dark eyelids
Bearing the golden bough of Argicida. So that:

Canto II

Hang it all, Robert Browning,
　　　　　there can be but the one 'Sordello'.
But Sordello, and my Sordello?
Lo Sordels si fo di Mantovana.
So-shu churned in the sea.
Seal sports in the spray-whited circles of cliff-wash,
Sleek head, daughter of Lir,
　　　　　eyes of Picasso
Under black fur-hood, lithe daughter of Ocean;
And the wave runs in the beach-groove:
'Eleanor, ἑλέναυς and ἑλέπτολις!'
　　　　　And poor old Homer blind, blind, as a bat,
Ear, ear for the sea-surge, murmur of old men's voices:
'Let her go back to the ships,
Back among Grecian faces, lest evil come on our own,
Evil and further evil, and a curse cursed on our children,
Moves, yes she moves like a goddess
And has the face of a god
　　　　　and the voice of Schoeney's daughters,
And doom goes with her in walking,
Let her go back to the ships,
　　　　　back among Grecian voices.'
That by the beach-run, Tyro,
　　　　　Twisted arms of the sea-god,
Lithe sinews of water, gripping her, cross-hold,
And the blue-gray glass of the wave tents them,
Glare azure of water, cold-welter, close cover.
Quiet sun-tawny sand-stretch,
The gulls broad out their wings,
　　　　　nipping between the splay feathers;
Snipe come for their bath,
　　　　　bend out their wing-joints,
Spread wet wings to the sun-film,

And by Scios,
      to left of the Naxos passage,
Naviform rock overgrown,
      algæ cling to its edge,
There is a wine-red glow in the shallows,
      a tin flash in the sun-dazzle.

The ship landed in Scios,
      men wanting spring-water,
And by the rock-pool a young boy loggy with vine-must,
      'To Naxos? Yes, we'll take you to Naxos,
Cum' along lad.' 'Not that way!'
'Aye, that way is Naxos.'
      And I said: 'It's a straight ship.'
And an ex-convict out of Italy
      knocked me into the fore-stays,
(He was wanted for manslaughter in Tuscany)
      And the whole twenty against me,
Mad for a little slave money.
      And they took her out of Scios
And off her course ...
      And the boy came to, again, with the racket,
And looked out over the bows,
      and to eastward, and to the Naxos passage.
God sleight then, god-sleight:
      Ship stock fast in sea-swirl,
Ivy upon the oars, King Pentheus,
      grapes with no seed but sea-foam,
Ivy in scupper-hole.
Aye, I, Acœtes, stood there,
      and the god stood by me,
Water cutting under the keel,
Sea-break from stern forrards,
      wake running off from the bow,
And where was gunwale, there now was vine-trunk,
And tenthril where cordage had been,

       grape-leaves on the rowlocks,
Heavy vine on the oarshafts,
And, out of nothing, a breathing,
       hot breath on my ankles,
Beasts like shadows in glass,
       a furred tail upon nothingness.
Lynx-purr, and heathery smell of beasts,
       where tar smell had been,
Sniff and pad-foot of beasts,
       eye-glitter out of black air.
The sky overshot, dry, with no tempest,
Sniff and pad-foot of beasts,
       fur brushing my knee-skin,
Rustle of airy sheaths,
       dry forms in the *æther*.
And the ship like a keel in ship-yard,
       slung like an ox in smith's sling,
Ribs stuck fast in the ways,
       grape-cluster over pin-rack,
       void air taking pelt.
Lifeless air become sinewed,
       feline leisure of panthers,
Leopards sniffing the grape shoots by scupper-hole,
Crouched panthers by fore-hatch,
And the sea blue-deep about us,
       green-ruddy in shadows,
And Lyæus: 'From now, Acœtes, my altars,
Fearing no bondage,
       Fearing no cat of the wood,
Safe with my lynxes,
       feeding grapes to my leopards,
Olibanum is my incense,
       the vines grow in my homage.'

The back-swell now smooth in the rudder-chains,
Black snout of a porpoise

where Lycabs had been,
Fish-scales on the oarsmen.
        And I worship.
I have seen what I have seen.
        When they brought the boy I said:
'He has a god in him,
        though I do not know which god.'
And they kicked me into the fore-stays.
I have seen what I have seen:
        Medon's face like the face of a dory,
Arms shrunk into fins. And you, Pentheus,
Had as well listen to Tiresias, and to Cadmus,
        or your luck will go out of you.
Fish-scales over groin muscles,
        lynx-purr amid sea . . .
And of a later year,
        pale in the wine-red algæ,
If you will lean over the rock,
        the coral face under wave-tinge,
Rose-paleness under water-shift,
        Ileuthyeria, fair Dafne of sea-bords,
The swimmer's arms turned to branches,
Who will say in what year,
        fleeing what band of tritons,
The smooth brows, seen, and half seen,
        now ivory stillness.

So-shu churned in the sea, So-shu also,
        using the long moon for a churn-stick . . .
Lithe turning of water,
        sinews of Poseidon,
Black azure and hyaline,
        glass wave over Tyro,
Close cover, unstillness,
        bright welter of wave-cords,
Then quiet water,

               quiet in the buff sands,
Sea-fowl stretching wing-joints,
               splashing in rock-hollows and sand-hollows
In the wave-runs by the half-dune;
Glass-glint of wave in the tide-rips against sunlight,
               pallor of Hesperus,
Grey peak of the wave,
               wave, colour of grape's pulp,

Olive grey in the near,
               far, smoke grey of the rock-slide,
Salmon-pink wings of the fish-hawk
               cast grey shadows in water,
The tower like a one-eyed great goose
               cranes up out of the olive-grove,

And we have heard the fauns chiding Proteus
               in the smell of hay under the olive-trees.
And the frogs singing against the fauns
               in the half-light.
And . . .

Canto XIII

Kung walked
     by the dynastic temple
and into the cedar grove,
     and then out by the lower river,
And with him Khieu Tchi
     and Tian the low speaking
And 'we are unknown,' said Kung,
'You will take up charioteering?
     Then you will become known,
Or perhaps I should take up charioteering, or archery?
Or the practice of public speaking?'
And Tseu-lou said, 'I would put the defences in order,'
And Khieu said, 'If I were lord of a province
I would put it in better order than this is.'
And Tchi said, 'I should prefer a small mountain temple,
With order in the observances,
     with a suitable performance of the ritual,'
And Tian said, with his hand on the strings of his lute
The low sounds continuing
     after his hand left the strings,
And the sound went up like smoke, under the leaves,
And he looked after the sound:
     'The old swimming hole,
And the boys flopping off the planks,
Or sitting in the underbrush playing mandolins.'
     And Kung smiled upon all of them equally.
And Thseng-sie desired to know:
     'Which had answered correctly?'
And Kung said, 'They have all answered correctly,
That is to say, each in his nature.'
And Kung raised his cane against Yuan Jang,
     Yuan Jang being his elder,
For Yuan Jang sat by the roadside pretending to

be receiving wisdom.
And Kung said
          'You old fool, come out of it,
Get up and do something useful.'
          And Kung said
'Respect a child's faculties
From the moment it inhales the clear air,
But a man of fifty who knows nothing
          Is worthy of no respect.'
And 'When the prince has gathered about him
All the savants and artists, his riches will be fully employed.'
And Kung said, and wrote on the bo leaves:
          'If a man have not order within him
He can not spread order about him;
And if a man have not order within him
His family will not act with due order;
          And if the prince have not order within him
He can not put order in his dominions.'
And Kung gave the words 'order'
and 'brotherly deference'
And said nothing of the 'life after death'.
And he said
          'Anyone can run to excesses,
It is easy to shoot past the mark,
It is hard to stand firm in the middle.'

And they said: 'If a man commit murder
          Should his father protect him, and hide him?'
And Kung said:
          'He should hide him.'

And Kung gave his daughter to Kong-Tchang
          Although Kong-Tchang was in prison
And he gave his niece to Nan-Young
          although Nan-Young was out of office.
And Kung said 'Wang ruled with moderation,
          In his day the State was well kept,

And even I can remember
A day when the historians left blanks in their writings,
I mean for things they didn't know,
But that time seems to be passing.'
And Kung said, 'Without character you will
      be unable to play on that instrument
Or to execute the music fit for the Odes.
The blossoms of the apricot
      blow from the east to the west,
And I have tried to keep them from falling.'

Canto XLV

With *Usura*

With usura hath no man a house of good stone
each block cut smooth and well fitting
that design might cover their face,
with usura
hath no man a painted paradise on his church wall
harpes et luz
or where virgin receiveth message
and halo projects from incision,
with usura
seeth no man Gonzaga his heirs and his concubines
no picture is made to endure nor to live with
but it is made to sell and sell quickly
with usura, sin against nature,
is thy bread ever more of stale rags
is thy bread dry as paper,
with no mountain wheat, no strong flour
with usura the line grows thick
with usura is no clear demarcation
and no man can find site for his dwelling.
Stonecutter is kept from his stone
weaver is kept from his loom
WITH USURA
wool comes not to market
sheep bringeth no gain with usura
Usura is a murrain, usura
blunteth the needle in the maid's hand
and stoppeth the spinner's cunning Pietro Lombardo
came not by usura
Duccio came not by usura
nor Pier della Francesca; Zuan Bellin' not by usura
nor was 'La Calunnia' painted.

Came not by usura Angelico; came not Ambrogio Praedis,
Came no church of cut stone signed: *Adamo me fecit.*
Not by usura St Trophime
Not by usura Saint Hilaire,
Usura rusteth the chisel
It rusteth the craft and the craftsman
It gnaweth the thread in the loom
None learneth to weave gold in her pattern;
Azure hath a canker by usura; cramoisi is unbroidered
Emerald findeth no Memling
Usura slayeth the child in the womb
It stayeth the young man's courting
It hath brought palsey to bed, lyeth
between the young bride and her bridegroom
                    CONTRA NATURAM
They have brought whores for Eleusis
Corpses are set to banquet
at behest of usura.

N.B. Usury: A charge for the use of purchasing power, levied without regard to production; often without regard to the possibilities of production. (Hence the failure of the Medici bank.)

Canto XLVII

Who even dead, yet hath his mind entire!
This sound came in the dark
First must thou go the road
                    to hell
And to the bower of Ceres' daughter Proserpine,
Through overhanging dark, to see Tiresias,
Eyeless that was, a shade, that is in hell
So full of knowing that the beefy men know less than he,
Ere thou come to thy road's end.
                    Knowledge the shade of a shade,
Yet must thou sail after knowledge
Knowing less than drugged beasts. *phtheggometha
thasson*
φθελλώμεθα θᾶσσον
          The small lamps drift in the bay
And the sea's claw gathers them.
Neptunus drinks after neap-tide.
Tamuz! Tamuz!!
The red flame going seaward.
          By this gate art thou measured.
From the long boats they have set lights in the water,
The sea's claw gathers them outward.
Scilla's dogs snarl at the cliff's base,
The white teeth gnaw in under the crag,
But in the pale night the small lamps float seaward
                              τυ Διώνα
                              TU DIONA

και Μοῖρα τ᾽ Ἄδονιν
KAI MOIRA T᾽ ADONIN

84

The sea is streaked red with Adonis,
The lights flicker red in small jars.
Wheat shoots rise new by the altar,
        flower from the swift seed.
Two span, two span to a woman,
Beyond that she believes not. Nothing is of any importance.
To that is she bent, her intention,
To that art thou called ever turning intention,
Whether by night the owl-call, whether by sap in shoot,
Never idle, by no means by no wiles intermittent
Moth is called over mountain
The bull runs blind on the sword, *naturans*
To the cave art thou called, Odysseus,
By Molü hast thou respite for a little,
By Molü art thou freed from the one bed
        that thou may'st return to another
The stars are not in her counting,
        To her they are but wandering holes.
Begin thy plowing
When the Pleiades go down to their rest,
Begin thy plowing
40 days are they under seabord,
Thus do in fields by seabord
And in valleys winding down toward the sea.
When the cranes fly high
        think of plowing.
By this gate art thou measured
Thy day is between a door and a door
Two oxen are yoked for plowing
Or six in the hill field
White bulk under olives, a score for drawing down stone,
Here the mules are gabled with slate on the hill road.
Thus was it in time.
And the small stars now fall from the olive branch,
Forked shadow falls dark on the terrace

More black than the floating martin
        that has no care for your presence,
His wing-print is black on the roof tiles
And the print is gone with his cry.
So light is thy weight on Tellus
Thy notch no deeper indented
Thy weight less than the shadow
Yet hast thou gnawed through the mountain,
        Scilla's white teeth less sharp.
Hast thou found a nest softer than cunnus
Or hast thou found better rest
Hast'ou a deeper planting, doth thy death year
Bring swifter shoot?
Hast thou entered more deeply the mountain?

The light has entered the cave. Io! Io!
The light has gone down into the cave,
Splendour on splendour!
By prong have I entered these hills:
That the grass grow from my body,
That I hear the roots speaking together,
The air is new on my leaf,
The forked boughs shake with the wind.
Is Zephyrus more light on the bough, Apeliota
more light on the almond branch?
By this door have I entered the hill.
Falleth,
Adonis falleth.
Fruit cometh after. The small lights drift out with the tide,
sea's claw has gathered them outward,
Four banners to every flower
The sea's claw draws the lamps outward.
Think thus of thy plowing
When the seven stars go down to their rest
Forty days for their rest, by seabord
And in valleys that wind down toward the sea

86

καὶ Μοῖρα τ᾽ Ἄδονιν
KAI MOIRA T' ADONIN
When the almond bough puts forth its flame,
When the new shoots are brought to the altar,
τυ Διῳνα, καὶ Μοῖρα
TU DIONA, KAI MOIRA
καὶ Μοῖρα τ᾽ Ἄδονιν
KAI MOIRA T' ADONIN
    that hath the gift of healing,
that hath the power over wild beasts.

Canto LI

Shines
in the mind of heaven   God
who made it
more than the sun
in our eye.
Fifth element; mud; said Napoleon
With usury has no man a good house
made of stone, no paradise on his church wall
With usury the stone cutter is kept from his stone
the weaver is kept from his loom by usura
Wool does not come into market
the peasant does not eat his own grain
The girl's needle goes blunt in her hand
The looms are hushed one after another
ten thousand after ten thousand
Duccio was not by usura
Nor was 'La Calunnia' painted.
Neither Ambrogio Praedis nor Angelico
had their skill by usura
Nor St Trophime its cloisters;
Nor St Hilaire its proportion.
Usury rusts the man and his chisel
It destroys the craftsman; destroying craft
Azure is caught with cancer. Emerald comes to no Memling
Usury kills the child in the womb
And breaks short the young man's courting
Usury brings age into youth; it lies between the bride
and the bridegroom
Usury is against Nature's increase.
Whores for Eleusis;
Under usury no stone is cut smooth
Peasant has no gain from his sheep herd
          Blue dun; number 2 in most rivers

for dark days; when it is cold
A starling's wing will give you the colour
or duck widgeon; if you take feather from under the wing
Let the body be of blue fox fur, or a water rat's
or grey squirrel's. Take this with a portion of mohair
and a cock's hackle for legs.
12th of March to 2nd of April
Hen pheasant's feather does for a fly,
green tail, the wings flat on the body
Dark fur from a hare's ear for a body
a green shaded partridge feather
        grizzled yellow cock's hackle
green wax; harl from a peacock's tail
bright lower body; about the size of pin
the head should be. can be fished from seven a.m.
till eleven; at which time the brown marsh fly comes on.
As long as the brown continues, no fish will take Granham

That hath the light of the doer; as it were
a form cleaving to it.
Deo similis quodam modo
hic intellectus adeptus
Grass; nowhere out of place. Thus speaking in Konigsberg
Zwischen die Volkern erzielt wird
a modus vivendi.
circling in eddying air; in a hurry;
the 12: close eyed in the oily wind
these were the regents; and a sour song from the folds
        of his belly
sang Geryone: I am the help of the aged;
I pay men to talk peace;
Mistress of many tongues; merchant of chalcedony
I am Geryon twin with usura,
You who have lived in a stage set.

A thousand were dead in his folds;
in the eel-fishers basket
Time was of the League of Cambrai:

from Canto LXXX

[Only shadows enter my tent
                as men pass between me and the sunset,]
beyond the eastern barbed wire
      a sow with nine boneen
matronly as any duchess at Claridge's

and for that Christmas at Maurie Hewlett's
Going out from Southampton
they passed the car by the dozen
        who would not have shown weight on a scale
                  riding, riding
                          for Noel the green holly
      Noel, Noel, the green holly
      A dark night for the holly

That would have been Salisbury plain, and I have not
      thought of
        the Lady Anne for this twelve years
              Nor of Le Portel
How tiny the panelled room where they stabbed him
          In her lap, almost, La Stuarda
          Si tuit li dolh ehl planh el marrimen
                for the leopards and broom plants

Tudor indeed is gone and every rose,
Blood-red, blanch-white that in the sunset glows
Cries: 'Blood, Blood, Blood!' against the gothic stone
Of England, as the Howard or Boleyn knows.

Nor seeks the carmine petal to infer;
Nor is the white bud Time's inquisitor
Probing to know if its new-gnarled root
Twists from York's head or belly of Lancaster;

Or if a rational soul should stir, perchance,
Within the stem or summer shoot to advance
Contrition's utmost throw, seeking in thee
But oblivion, not thy forgiveness, FRANCE.

as the young lizard extends his leopard spots
        along the grass-blade seeking the green midge half an
            ant-size
and the Serpentine will look just the same
and the gulls be as neat on the pond
and the sunken garden unchanged
and God knows what else is left of our London
            my London, your London
and if her green elegance
        remains on this side of my rain ditch
        puss lizard will lunch on some other T-bone

sunset grand couturier.

from Canto LXXXI

Ed ascoltando al leggier mormorio
     there came new subtlety of eyes into my tent,
whether of spirit or hypostasis,
     but what the blindfold hides
or at carneval
                         nor any pair showed anger
     Saw but the eyes and stance between the eyes,
colour, diastasis,
     careless or unaware it had not the
  whole tent's room
nor was place for the full Ειδώς
interpass, penetrate
     casting but shade beyond the other lights
          sky's clear
          night's sea
          green of the mountain pool
          shone from the unmasked eyes in half-mask's
               space.
What thou lovest well remains,
                              the rest is dross
What thou lov'st well shall not be reft from thee
What thou lov'st well is thy true heritage
Whose world, or mine or theirs
                         or is it of none?
First came the seen, then thus the palpable
     Elysium, though it were in the halls of hell,
What thou lovest well is thy true heritage
What thou lov'st well shall not be reft from thee

The ant's a centaur in his dragon world.
Pull down thy vanity, it is not man
Made courage, or made order, or made grace,
     Pull down thy vanity, I say pull down.

Learn of the green world what can be thy place
In scaled invention or true artistry,
Pull down thy vanity,

                    Paquin pull down!
The green casque has outdone your elegance.

'Master thyself, then others shall thee beare'
    Pull down thy vanity
Thou art a beaten dog beneath the hail,
A swollen magpie in a fitful sun,
Half black half white
Nor knowst'ou wing from tail
Pull down thy vanity
          How mean thy hates
Fostered in falsity,
         Pull down thy vanity,
Rathe to destroy, niggard in charity,
Pull down thy vanity,
         I say pull down.

But to have done instead of not doing
         this is not vanity
To have, with decency, knocked
That a Blunt should open
      To have gathered from the air a live tradition
or from a fine old eye the unconquered flame
This is not vanity.
     Here error is all in the not done,
all in the diffidence that faltered.

from Canto LXXXIII

    and Brother Wasp is building a very neat house
    of four rooms, one shaped like a squat indian bottle
    La vespa, *la* vespa, mud, swallow system
so that dreaming of Bracelonde and of Perugia
and the great fountain in the Piazza
or of old Bulagaio's cat that with a well timed leap
    could turn the lever-shaped door handle
It comes over me that Mr Walls must be a ten-strike
with the signorinas
and in the warmth after chill sunrise
an infant, green as new grass,
has stuck its head or tip
out of Madame La Vespa's bottle

mint springs up again
    in spite of Jones' rodents
as had the clover by the gorilla cage
    with a four-leaf

When the mind swings by a grass-blade
    an ant's forefoot shall save you
the clover leaf smells and tastes as its flower

    The infant has descended,
    from mud on the tent roof to Tellus,
like to like colour he goes amid grass-blades
    greeting them that dwell under XTHONOS   ΧΘΟΝΟΣ
ΟΙ ΧΘΟΝΙΟΙ; to carry our news
      εἰς χθονιους to them that dwell under the earth
begotten of air, that shall sing in the bower
    of Kore,   Περσεφόνεια
and have speech with Tiresias, Thebae
Cristo Re, Dio Sole

in about $\frac{1}{2}$ a day she has made her adobe
(la vespa) the tiny mud-flask

    and that day I wrote no further

From Canto CXV

The scientists are in terror
            and the European mind stops
Wyndham Lewis chose blindness
            rather than have his mind stop.
Night under wind mid garofani,
            the petals are almost still
Mozart, Linnaeus, Sulmona,
When one's friends hate each other
            how can there be peace in the world?
Their asperities diverted me in my green time.
A blown husk that is finished
            but the light sings eternal
a pale flare over marshes
            where the salt hay whispers to tide's change
Time, space,
            neither life nor death is the answer.
And of man seeking good,
            doing evil.
In meiner Heimat
            where the dead walked
                  and the living were made of cardboard.